Big Bad Bug

WRITTEN BY
VIVIAN FRENCH
ILLUSTRATED BY
EMILY BOLAM

WALKER BOOKS
AND SUBSIDIARIES
LONDON • BOSTON • SYDNEY

First published 2001 by Walker Books Ltd
87 Vauxhall Walk, London SE11 5HJ

2 4 6 8 10 9 7 5 3 1

Text © 2001 Vivian French
Illustrations © 2001 Emily Bolam

This book has been typeset in Century Old Style.

Printed in Hong Kong

British Library Cataloguing in Publication Data
A catalogue record for this book is
available from the British Library.

ISBN 0-7445-6899-4

Notes for Children

This book is a little different from other picture books.
You will be sharing it with other people and telling
the story together.

You can read

this line

this line

or this line.

Even when someone else is reading, try to follow
the words. It will help when it's your turn!

Bee

Buzz!

We see a bee

Buzz!

We see one bee

Buzz!

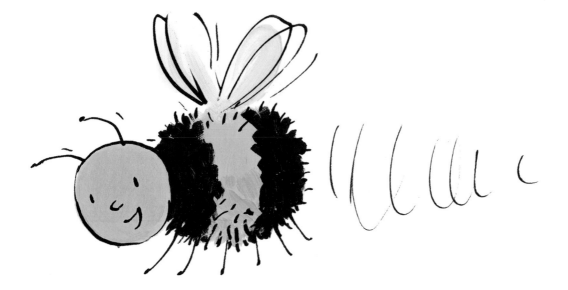

We see two bees

Buzz! Buzz!

We see a big bee

Buzz!

We see a little bee

Bizz!

Bug

Zizz!

We see a bug

Zizz!

We see a big bug

Zizz!

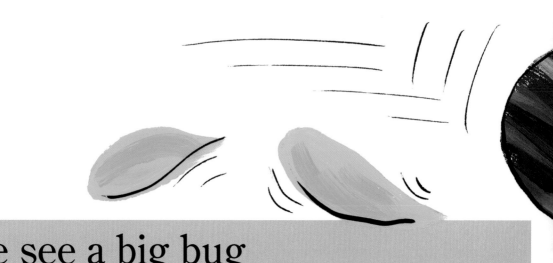

We see a big bug

Wizz!

We see a bad bug

Wizz! Wizz!

We see a big bad bug

Wizz! Wizz! Wizz!

Tree

Oooh!

We see a tree

Oooh!

We see a tall tree

Oooh!

We see a tall tall tree

Oooh!

We see a little bee

Bizz!

A little bee on the tall tall tree

Bizz! Bizz! Bizz!

Look!

Here comes bug

Big bad bug

Wizz!

Big bad bug flies to the tree

Wizz! Wizz! Wizz!

Big bad bug on the tall tree

Big bad bug and little bee

Wizz! Wizz! Wizz!

Bizz! Bizz! Bizz!

Oh!

Oh!

Look!

Here comes bee

Big bee

Buzz!

Big bee flies to the tall tall tree

Buzz! Buzz! Buzz!

BU*ZZZZZZZZZZZZZZZZZZZ*!!!

Oh!

No bug

No bad bug

No big bad bug

No bad bug on the tall tall tree.

Big bee

Buzz!

Little bee

Bizz!

Buzz! Bizz!

No wizz!

Little bee flies away

Big bee flies away

One tall tall tree

No bizz!

No buzz!

No wizz!

Notes for Teachers

Story Plays are written and presented in a way that encourages children to read aloud together. They are exciting stories, told in strongly patterned language which gives children the chance to practise at a vital stage of their reading development. Sharing stories in this way makes reading an active and enjoyable process, and one that draws in even the reticent reader.

The story is told by three different voices, divided into three colours so that each child can easily read his or her part. When there are more than three children in a group, there is an ideal opportunity for paired reading. Partnering a more experienced reader with a less experienced one can be very supportive and provides a learning experience for both children.

Story Plays encourage children to share in the reading of a whole text in a collaborative and interactive way. This makes them perfect for group and guided reading activities. Children will find they need to pay close attention to the print and punctuation, and to use the meaning of the whole story in order to read it with expression and a real sense of voice.